Welcome Aboard

Welcome Aboard

Copyright © 2001 Fergus Ryan

This edition copyright © Ichthus Communications

First Edition 2001

ISBN 1-904093-00-0

Published by Ichthus Communications
7 Greenwich Quay, Clarence Road, Greenwich, London SE8 3EY

For more information about the Headway Discipleship Series

In Britain contact Ichthus Communications:
tel. 020 8699 4208 or 020 8694 7171
email: admin@ichthus.org.uk
www.ichthus.org.uk

In Ireland contact FBC:
email: info@fbc.ie
www.fbc.ie

In Scotland contact The Network Churches:
tel. 0141 762 1473
email: info@shipcc.org.uk

All rights reserved. No part of this publication may be reproduced, stored in a retrieval system, or transmitted in any form or by any means, electronic, mechanical, photocopying, recording or otherwise, without the prior permission of the publisher.

Scripture quotations taken from the HOLY BIBLE,
NEW INTERNATIONAL VERSION.
Copyright © 1973, 1978, 1984 by International Bible Society.
Used by permission.

Illustrations copyright © 2001 by Sarah McIntyre
All rights reserved

Cover and book design: pool 31 (Jonathan Kearney)

Welcome Aboard

Contents

A Personal Note		4
Foreword by Roger T Forster		5
Introduction		6

Week 1: Knowing God 10
Day 1:   God is Your Father 12
Day 2:   Jesus the Centre of Everything 14
Day 3:   Listening to God: The Bible 16
Day 4:   Listening to God: The Spirit 18
Day 5:   Listening to God: A Quiet Place 20

Week 2: Freedom in Jesus 22
Day 1:   Freedom From Guilt 24
Day 2:   Strongholds in Your Life 26
Day 3:   Sleeping With the Enemy 28
Day 4:   Demolishing Strongholds 30
Day 5:   The Uniform of the Kingdom 32

Week 3: The Kingdom of God 34
Day 1:   The Jesus Manifesto 36
Day 2:   The Presence of the Future 38
Day 3:   Mission Impossible 40
Day 4:   The Community of the King 42
Day 5:   Your Kingdom Birthright 44

Week 4: The Word of God 46
Day 1:   God's Powerful Word 48
Day 2:   Modern Versions 50
Day 3:   Reading the Bible for Yourself 52
Day 4:   Spending an Hour in Prayer 54
Day 5:   The Way Ahead 56

Welcome Aboard

A Personal Note

Before taking early retirement in 1993, much of my life had been spent in intercontinental navigation. Unlike the more nautical theme of this Headway Discipleship Series, however, my journeys were aeronautical. Long-haul flying afforded me the privilege of meeting and worshipping with followers of Jesus in North America, the Caribbean, Africa and the Middle East, as well as all over Europe. When Eastern Europe first opened up to Western overflights I prayed for believers and those seeking God in the cities visible 35,000 feet below (I called it 'prayer-bombing'!) – cities from which stories of Christian suffering, heroism and overcoming had emerged in the preceding decades, and in which there now seemed to be the brightening air of a new morning.

My aerial version of prayer-walking came to be focused most often on South-East London, over which we frequently circled in holding patterns, awaiting our approach clearance to Gatwick or Heathrow. Below were many of the congregations of Ichthus Christian Fellowship, led by Roger and Faith Forster. From the 'heavenlies' I prayed for their ministry and mission, for to Roger and Faith and their companions I owe much of my understanding of the themes of Jesus' kingdom here represented in the Headway Series. They have not only taught these things, but they have modelled them in spirit and in action. In a sense I am returning in my own packaging what is already theirs. I am grateful for their help in reading and correcting the final text in the Series, and for some additional material in Making Headway by Roger. Also from Ichthus, Ken McGreavy many times helped our leadership team in Dublin to keep Jesus at 'the centre' and to work out our calling in practice, and Simon Thomas helped us do it all in the Holy Spirit and with much fun! Sarah McIntyre has done the wonderful artwork which gives the Series its 'people' focus, and Jonathan Kearney has brought the text to life with his creative and user-friendly design and layout. It was a pleasure working with him.

I am continually grateful too for the support and witness of my teammate Paul Rothwell and the radically committed believers who lead the cell groups and various ministries of FBC in Dublin, including my wife Sarah. Without their Spirit-filled and sacrificial ministry for the kingdom the teachings of this Series might have remained, for us at least, in the realm of theory.

Fergus Ryan
Dublin, Midsummer's Day, 2001

Welcome Aboard

Foreword by Roger T Forster

Jesus said, 'You shall know the truth and the truth shall set you free.' These words are the motivation behind the Headway Discipleship Series written by Fergus Ryan. Fergus has assimilated, shaped and set down material from preaching, tapes and books flowing from myself and from my colleagues in Ichthus, and has added to it his own fresh insights. He has also drawn on teachings from other backgrounds and traditions. The resulting compilation, distilled into manageable, bite-sized portions, is here in these manuals.

The subjects range from basic Christian doctrine to deepest theological reflection. The liberating, exhilarating power of the truth has set our own hearts aflame. It is our earnest prayer that it may do the same for you through these pages, whether you are a new disciple of Jesus or have walked with him for many years. If you are to grow in your relationship with him then you need to know 'the exact truth of the things you have been instructed in . . .' as Luke reminds us at the beginning of his Gospel.

Jesus commanded us to make disciples of ourselves and others and the beginning of discipleship is 'revelation and response'. The two 'disciples on the Emmaus road' (Luke 24) found their hearts burning within them as Jesus opened the Scriptures to them and showed them the truth about himself. Then their eyes were opened and they saw Jesus breaking the bread for them. As Jesus becomes clearer to us through our study of the Scriptures, our hearts will respond in love and worship. We will then find that Jesus himself is feeding the bread to us, and we will hear his voice and see his glory. This is why Paul prayed for the Ephesians that 'the God and Father of our Lord Jesus Christ, the Father of Glory, may give you a spirit of wisdom and revelation in the full knowledge of him' (Ephesians 1:17).

As we understand more deeply the faith we profess, we are also more able to relate relevantly to our current so-called 'post-Christian' society and culture. Jesus is the truth for all time and all times, and there are answers in him to the questions people ask as they seek to steer through the turbulent seas of our day. Better disciples will be better able to challenge the attitudes and assumptions of our society with a confidence that has discovered the riches of wisdom in Jesus.

These studies are designed to help us love God with all our heart, soul, mind and strength, and to overflow with love for others that will motivate us to share the truth with them. Join us in this adventure which will last not just for a lifetime but for eternity.

Roger T Forster
London, UK

introduction
Welcome Aboard!

If you have decided to follow Jesus Christ, then this book is just for you. It is designed as the first 'port of call' in a journey with him in which it is his great desire to bless you, and to equip you to be a blessing to others.

MEETING THE CAPTAIN...

So that you won't feel 'at sea', this booklet helps you to get to know the Master, the Lord Jesus, to know his voice, and to begin to experience the freedom he brings to those who follow him. It may seem like a paradox at first, but the greatest freedom is found in submission to Jesus.

...AND THE CREW

No one can make this journey alone; we all need the rest of the 'crew'. It is best if this booklet is used in the context of a cell group of about 8–15 people. Through loving and helping one another, and through learning by doing, they will become your new Christian 'family'. Here you can be nurtured in the journey in which Jesus wants to use you in his kingdom.

If you're not already in a cell group, talk to the person who gave you this book or to one of the leaders in your local Christian fellowship. There may be a cell group near you and the cell group leader will help you in deciding if you would like to join.

GETTING TO KNOW THE ROPES

Welcome Aboard is divided into four weekly sections with five days each. Each week you complete one section on your own, and then you could meet with a 'helper' from the cell group to go over what you have learned. Your helper's task is to encourage you in your relationship with Jesus, to pray for you, and to help you 'get to know the ropes' – the basic principles of life in Jesus' kingdom. You will be an encouragement to him or her too. These 'one-to-one' times will often be a highlight of your week.

SHIP'S MANUAL – THE BIBLE

You will discover very soon (if you have not done so already) that the Bible is a living and powerful resource, giving you strength and direction. It is as though the very breath of God is in your own mouth as you learn his Word. Memorising key verses of Scripture will help to equip you in taking hold of the blessings of God's kingdom, and in resisting the attacks and temptations of Satan. Since you have left *his* kingdom, he is going to try to divert you from following Jesus. You're probably aware of that yourself.

Jesus faced a temptation from the devil to be diverted from declaring and demonstrating God's kingdom. You can read about this in the Gospel of Matthew, chapter 4. You will face the same temptation to deny God's kingdom and to follow the values of this world. As Jesus always lived in the power of the Holy Spirit, he repelled Satan with the powerful weapon of God's Word. Satan even tried to twist that Word himself. Memorising Scripture allows you to draw on God's Word, even when you don't have a Bible with you. And the Holy Spirit in you will remind you what to say.

So right now begin to learn your first memory verse. It's from the First Letter of John, chapter 5, verses 11 and 12. Write it on a little card and try to learn it 'Word-perfect'. See if you can remember it when you meet your helper.

And this is the testimony: God has given us eternal life, and this life is in his Son. He who has the Son has life; he who does not have the Son of God does not have life. (1 John 5:11–12)

introduction | Welcome Aboard

Does this make sense yet? Write down some of the things you want to see happen in your life

By the way, if you haven't got a Bible yet, you should get a modern version such as New International Version (NIV), New American Standard Bible (NASB), New Revised Standard Version (NRSV), or the New King James Version. In the fourth week we'll look more closely at reading the Bible.

THE SHIP'S MISSION

As you begin this journey with Jesus as your Captain, let's look ahead to the mission for which he is equipping us. You don't need to grasp everything just now, but here's a helpful picture to give you a glimpse of some other 'ports of call' en-route and what the objective of each leg of the journey is.

JESUS THE CENTRE

Notice the cross on the sail in the centre. The Lord Jesus is the centre and purpose of everything we do. He is our life, our model, our Captain, our companion, our reward. Our purpose is to know him and to make him known. Knowing him is the main focus of *Welcome Aboard*.

H.E.L.L.O.

This little memory aid sums up your cell group's life and principal areas of activity. With Jesus as the centre and his Holy Spirit guiding you, you will express your life together in three ways: 1) community (or relationship), 2) discipleship (or training) and 3) mission to the world around us. *HELLO* helps us remember these elements of cell life: **H**eart for **E**vangelism, **L**earning together, **L**oving one another with Jesus' love, and **O**penness to the Holy Spirit.

When you have completed this booklet, *Welcome Aboard*, you'll receive *Making Headway*, the second stage of your discipleship journey. This will equip you in the values of the Christian life, in overcoming evil, in growing as part of a Christian community, and in discovering how God's Spirit releases special gifts in your life.

Later you'll receive *Ship's Mission*, the third stage of your journey, which focuses on Jesus' love for the world in its sorrows and sins. You will learn to show his kingdom to others in words, works and in the Spirit's power.

So that's a glance ahead, and now you're ready to begin. Tomorrow, turn to Week 1, Day 1 and we'll meet the Captain. Oh, and don't forget to thank him for pulling you out of a raging sea. You probably didn't get on at a port!

Pier
7
CRUISE
SPECIAL OFFERS
Summer Cruise Special
All-Day Cruise

week 1
Knowing God

day 1: God is Your Father

day 2: Jesus the Centre of Everything

day 3: Listening to God: the Bible

day 4: Listening to God: the Spirit

day 5: Listening to God: a Quiet Place

week 1
Knowing God

day 1: God is Your Father

When the Apostle John wrote the letter from which you have been learning your first memory verse, he was overwhelmed with the realisation of an amazing truth:

> *How great is the love the Father has lavished on us, that we should be called children of God! And that is what we are!*
> *(1 John 3:1)*

How do you think a person becomes a child of God?

- [ ] Everyone is a child of God naturally.
- [ ] No one is actually a child of God; they're adopted and legally regarded as sons and heirs.
- [ ] When I believe in and receive Jesus, Father's life is in me; I really become his child.
- [ ] I give up. Has it got something to do with baptism?

Now read this verse carefully:

> *Yet to all who received him [Jesus], to those who believed in his name, he gave the right to become children of God – children born not of natural descent, nor of human decision or a husband's will, but* **born of God**. *(John 1:12,13)*

Now this is a marvellous thing: when you believed in Jesus, gave your old life to him and repented of your sin, he did more than just forgive you (though that's a pretty earth-shattering fact in itself!). God even did much more than adopt you into his family. Perhaps in your earthly family you have been adopted. Hopefully, your new parents loved you, gave you everything you needed, and now legally you are their heir. But when you came to Jesus it was even better than that. God sent his Holy Spirit to you and put new life into you – his life. He fathered you. You have been born again! Peter said it like this:

> *For you have been born again, not of perishable seed, but of imperishable, through the living and enduring word of God.*
> *(1 Peter 1:23)*

Take a moment here to tell Father how you feel about that. If it helps, write down your feelings, but make sure you talk to Father too.

day 1 God is Your Father

WHAT FATHER FEELS ABOUT YOU

Your ideas of a father will have been formed largely by your relationship with your earthly father. You may feel loved and secure, or sadly, you may feel scorned or rejected. Well, there's some truly good news for you. God, who has *fathered* you in bringing you to share in his life, knows everything about you – your deepest, darkest secrets, your sorrows and disappointments, your hopes and longings. Yet he loves you deeply, he sent Jesus to salvage your life, and he longs to bless you.

Look up this verse in your own Bible and underline it. It's in the Old Testament book of Zephaniah:

> *The LORD your God is with you, he is mighty to save. He will take great delight in you, he will quiet you with his love, he will rejoice over you with singing. (Zephaniah 3:17)*

Have you ever thought of God taking delight in you? Here's another well-known verse about God's love:

> *For God so loved the world that he gave his one and only Son, that whoever believes in him shall not perish but have eternal life. (John 3:16)*

Definitely underline this in your Bible too.

How have you thought of God in the past – distant and harsh, or an old softie who overlooks wrong, or that he doesn't exist, or perhaps something else?

God is not only *fatherly* to you, he is also your Lord, your King. Everything that is good in the universe comes from God. Choosing to follow another way is foolishness and brings sorrow. It also gives ground for your enemy to spoil things. If we don't come and ask for forgiveness, our Father will lovingly bring us face to face with the consequences of choosing wrong paths.

Is Father speaking to your heart just now about anything? Spend time now with him. If you have a few minutes today, get alone and read out Psalm 139 as a prayer to your Father. You'll begin to learn to 'pray Scripture'.

13

week 1
Knowing God

day 2: Jesus the Centre of Everything

Perhaps you have heard about Jesus all your life. But when you were 'born of God', something amazing happened in you of which, at first, you may only grasp a little. As time goes by, the wonder of it will increase. *Jesus has, by his Holy Spirit, come to live his life in you and through you.*

Open your Bible to Galatians 2:20 and mark these words:

> *I have been crucified with Christ and I no longer live, but Christ lives in me. The life I live in the body, I live by faith in the Son of God, who loved me and gave himself for me.*

Now look at a longer passage in John's Gospel, chapter 14, verses 15–24. Who does it say lives in you?

Just for now, don't worry if you can't grasp how God can exist as three 'persons'. People much wiser than us have had difficulty finding the right words. Anyway, the Bible teaches that the Father is God, the Son is God and the Holy Spirit is God, and yet they are One. There is only one true God.

For the moment there are two things you should know. The first, as we have just seen, is that Jesus lives in you by his Holy Spirit. The second is this. *If we want to know God, we look at Jesus*, because Jesus is . . .

> *the radiance of God's glory and the exact representation of his being, sustaining all things by his powerful word. (Hebrews 1:3)*

When Jesus was on earth he showed what the Father is like, and he did the Father's works. The four Gospels are like a 'family picture album'. When we see Jesus, we see the exact likeness of the Father. One time Philip, a disciple of Jesus, asked him to show them the Father. Look up Jesus' reply in John's Gospel, chapter 14, verses 8 – 11. In what two things does Jesus say the Father is shown in his life?

• In his w _____ (see v 10)

• In his w _____

14

day 2 **Jesus the Centre of Everything**

The things that Jesus said, and the wonderful things he did were what Father was saying and doing. He was bringing the Kingdom of Heaven to the earth, and showing what happens when God is 'kinging it' (Roger Forster's phrase). Look up this verse in Acts in your own Bible:

> *God anointed Jesus of Nazareth with the Holy Spirit and power, and . . . he went around doing good and healing all who were under the power of the devil, because God was with him. (Acts 10:38)*

What three things enabled Jesus to do the Father's works?

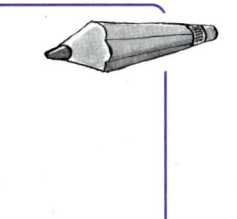

Look again at the verse; how does it describe what Jesus did?

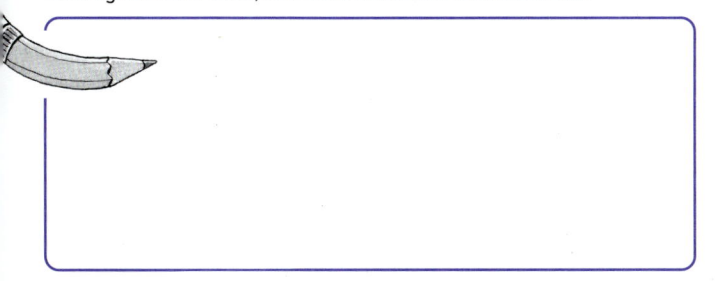

THE HOLY SPIRIT AND POWER

Jesus wants everyone in the world to be rescued from the works of the devil and to be delivered into the kingdom of God. The Holy Spirit has been given so that we can continue bringing God's kingdom to everyone.

> *I tell you the truth, anyone who has faith in me will do what I have been doing. He will do even greater things than these, because I am going to the Father. And I will ask the Father, and he will give you another Counsellor to be with you for ever – the Spirit of truth. The world cannot accept him, because it neither sees him nor knows him. But you know him, for he lives with you and will be in you. (John 14:12,16,17)*

Since God is in us, this means that the Holy Spirit is in us. The Holy Spirit always brings Jesus into view; he is called 'the Spirit of Christ'. Jesus is the centre, the focus of everything we do, because his life is in us.

Well, you'll have a lot more amazing things to learn about Jesus as we go along. Do you feel you're getting to know God a little better?

> Finally, review your memory verse, 1 John 5:11 and 12. Can you get it 'Word-perfect' yet?

week 1
Knowing God

day 3: Listening to God: the Bible

THE GOD WHO SPEAKS

Around the time the Bible was written, the Greeks had an idea of 'God' (the Deity) as far away, uninvolved in and unmoved by anything happening in the world. He didn't *care* in any sense. That God should *speak* was not considered consistent with his nature. That God could ever *come to the earth* was inconceivable.

That's a long way from the loving Father heart of God as revealed by Jesus. Consider this passage:

> *When [Jesus] saw the crowds, he had compassion on them, because they were harassed and helpless, like sheep without a shepherd. (Matthew 9:36)*

If you have a little extra time today, stop now and read John chapter 10:1–15. Allow God to speak to you through his Word. Then respond to him as you hear his voice. Do you feel *secure, trustful*, having Jesus as your Shepherd, the One who protects you from your enemy, the 'thief'?

Did you sense God speaking to you as you read from John chapter 10 (or Psalm 139, two days ago)? Was there something that seemed to 'leap out of the page' and you said, 'That's it, Lord; that's just for me'? Is that God speaking? Write down anything you felt God emphasising to you.

THE BIBLE – GOD'S LIVING WORD

The Bible says many times that its words are the words of God, breathed into its writers' hearts by the Holy Spirit.

> *Above all, you must understand that no prophecy of Scripture [i.e. the Bible] came about by the prophet's own interpretation. For prophecy never had its origin in the will of man, but men spoke from God as they were carried along by the Holy Spirit. (2 Peter 1:20,21)*

> *All Scripture is God-breathed . . . (2 Timothy 3:16)*

day 3 Listening to God: the Bible

The same Spirit who inspired the writers of the Bible lives in you. He speaks to your *mind*, helping to cast light on the truths in the Bible, developing your understanding of true doctrine. He also speaks to your *heart*, warning, correcting, guiding, building your faith.

God never contradicts his Word, so if impressions or thoughts come which are in conflict with Scripture, they are from somewhere other than God.

THE VOICE OF A STRANGER

So then, what if you are listening for God's voice and a thought contrary to the teaching of Scripture comes into your mind; what do you think its source might be? Mark any of the following you think could be true:

- [ ] Just a random thought from my mind.
- [ ] Mixed motives suggesting what I want to hear.
- [ ] Ideas from my past out of tune with God's Word.
- [ ] An evil spirit seeking to influence me.
- [ ] False teachings I picked up somewhere.

Actually, it could be any of these. There are some ways in which we can test what truly comes from the Father's heart. Have a look at these:

Look at the Bible. It is given to keep us from error. Read other sections of Scripture; the Bible is its own best interpreter. (We'll look at this again in Week 4.)

Look at Jesus and say, 'Is this like you, Lord?' The enemy often tries to oppose Jesus, his divinity, his virgin birth, his work on the cross, his resurrection. Or suggests something he would never do. For example:

> *Dear friends, do not believe every spirit, but test the spirits to see whether they are from God ... Every spirit that acknowledges that Jesus Christ has come in the flesh is from God.* (1 John 4:1–3)

Look in your heart for warning signals, a 'check' in your spirit. Is there peace or uncertainty?

Look to other Christians, your cell leader or a leader in the fellowship. The Lord gives teachers to help us. But even they are *subject* to God's Word, not *above* it. Nobody is infallible (i.e. without the possibility of making a mistake). Even the Apostle Peter was rebuked by the Apostle Paul for teaching error (Galatians 2:11–14)! And one group was praised for checking out in the Scriptures what Paul was saying (Acts 17:10,11). In Week 4 we'll look at study materials which will help you in understanding the Bible.

17

week 1
Knowing God

day 4: Listening to God: the Holy Spirit

Before we begin today, review your memory passage, First Letter of John, chapter 5, verses 11 and 12. Look at the next verse (13) and try adding it to the other two:

> *I write these things to you who believe in the name of the Son of God so that you may **know** that you have eternal life.*

THE SPIRIT AND THE WORD

As important as the Bible is for hearing God speak, some people have studied the Bible in theological college or in private for years and missed its central purpose. Jesus often *confronted* the religious leaders of his day, calling them 'blind guides' who knew neither the Scriptures nor the power of God, having only a 'formal' godliness. He told them:

> *You diligently study the Scriptures because you think that by them you possess eternal life. These are the Scriptures that testify about me, yet you refuse to come to me to have life. (John 5:39–40)*

The centre of our faith is not the Bible itself, but *Jesus*.

God's Word is like a signpost pointing unerringly to Jesus. Lots of people analyse the signpost, study its letters, the language used, its origin, and yet somehow miss experiencing the very One it is pointing to. Imagine a group of people gathered to study a sign that said 'Apple pie 5 metres' while the apple pie sat there uneaten! The Spirit who inspired the Word leads us to Jesus himself. Psalm 34:8 says, 'Taste and see that the Lord is good!'

God's Word is also like the headlights of a car. The lights themselves are neither the way nor the destination; they light up the way.

> *Your word is a lamp to my feet and a light for my path. (Psalm 119:105)*

Jesus is both the Way, and – with the Father – the Goal.

> *I am the way and the truth and the life. No one comes to the Father except through me. (John 14:6)*

So how is it that the way that seems so obvious to you now that you have become a Christian seems so unclear even to religious people? Any ideas?

day 4 **Listening to God: the Holy Spirit**

Consider this verse carefully.

> *The man without the Spirit does not accept the things that come from the Spirit of God, for they are foolishness to him, and he cannot understand them, because they are spiritually discerned.* (1 Corinthians 2:14)

Jesus told us that the truth of Scripture can really only be understood through the same Spirit who authored it. Some scholars deny that the Bible is from the Spirit at all. Clearly, Jesus wouldn't have agreed with them.

Look at these promises Jesus gave his followers:

> *I will ask the Father, and he will give you another Counsellor to be with you for ever – the Spirit of truth. The world cannot accept him, because it neither sees him nor knows him. But you know him, for he lives with you and will be in you. I will not leave you as orphans; I will come to you.* (John 14:16–18)

> *But when he, the Spirit of truth, comes, he will guide you into all truth . . . He will bring glory to me by taking from what is mine and making it known to you.* (John 16:13,14)

Read over these verses and note what you've learned about the Holy Spirit.

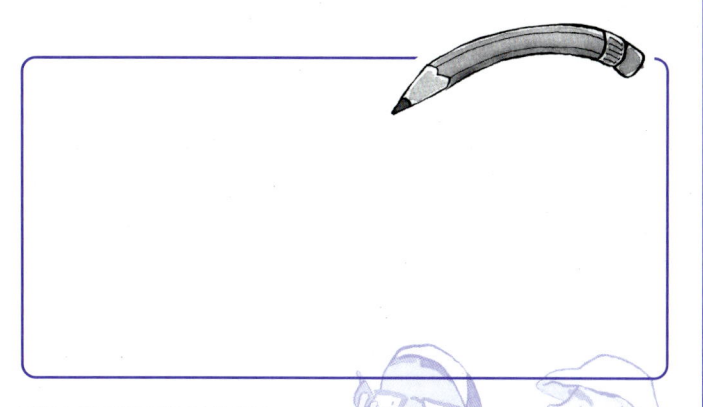

THE SPIRIT'S VOICE

Sometimes the Holy Spirit gives us a *picture in our minds*; this happened many times in the Bible (e.g. Jeremiah 1:11–14). God has often communicated in a *dream*. Then there are *ideas, words* or *warnings* that did not come from our own minds. Occasionally the Lord might bring particular *persons* to mind so that we will pray for them, or some *information* we cannot have known naturally. We still need wisdom in testing what is truly from God, or whether his message is to be *prayed about* or *shared with someone else*. We need the Lord's *timing*. Above all, be alert to the temptation to try to look 'spiritual' to others (it's just pride), or worse still, to try to manipulate or control them by saying 'the Lord told me'. Always be humble and gentle. Ask your leaders to help you and take note of their counsel.

week 1
Knowing God

day 5: Listening to God: a Quiet Place

Sometimes if you're standing in a great cathedral you may be filled with a sense of awe or beauty. God is certainly awesome and beautiful. But you may feel the same sense of majesty at great sea cliffs, and be reminded of the amazing creative power of God. There are no special places where God meets you; you can talk to him upstairs on the bus or on the local train on the way to work. But most times we will want to be alone with God in a quiet place. Jesus often withdrew from the crowds and the noise to be alone with the Father. Luke 5:16 tells us:

Jesus often withdrew to lonely places and prayed.

YOUR OWN QUIET PLACE

Father is eager to meet with you. You've probably already found yourself looking for a quiet place to spend time following these notes. Decide now whether there is a time and a place where you can be alone with the Father every day. This is going to become a very special part of your life.

Are there any changes you would have to make to your schedule to give priority to this time with God? Think about morning or evening, hobbies, TV, work pattern, time with your family. Write down what you've decided to do:

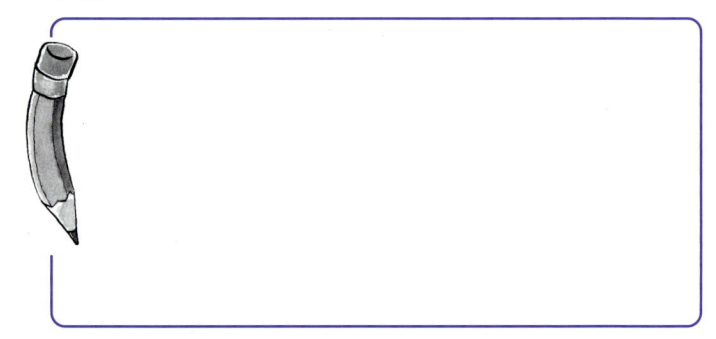

If you received an invitation to a celebrity dinner you probably wouldn't let anything disrupt your plans! What kinds of things might interrupt your time with God?

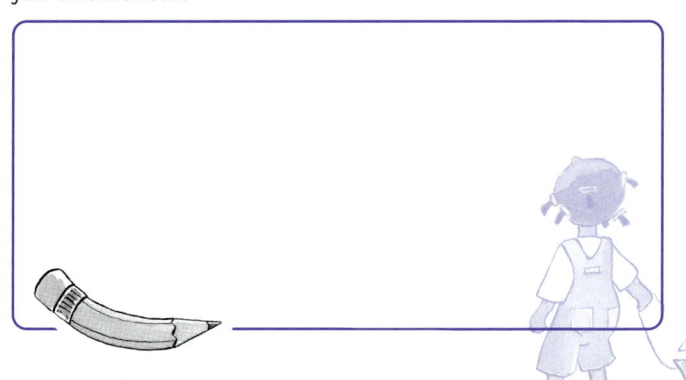

day 5   Listening to God: a Quiet Place

Consider using the car, a beach, a park, a quiet room in the house. By the way, *you* don't have to be quiet! You can sing and worship God with a praise CD. You could lie flat, kneel, move around, shout, cry, whisper or be silent.

What kinds of things could you do to eliminate or minimise interruptions in your 'quiet place'?

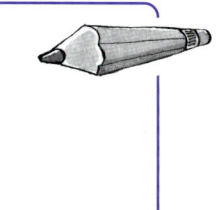

STREAMS OF BLESSING

Your times with Father, far from being a duty, should be times when your thirst is quenched, your heart refreshed, and you receive new strength. Here's your invitation from Isaiah 55:1,2:

> *Come, all you who are thirsty, come to the waters; and you who have no money, come, buy and eat! Come, buy wine and milk without money and without cost. Why spend money on what is not bread, and your labour on what does not satisfy? Listen, listen to me, and eat what is good, and your soul will delight in the richest of fare.*

As I was writing this very page, the telephone rang, and one of our cell group leaders, unaware of what I was doing, told me the Lord had given her this word for me:

> *Blessed is the man who listens to me, watching daily at my doors, waiting at my doorway. (Proverbs 8:34)*

Isn't that just like Father?

JOURNALING YOUR JOURNEY

This week has been all about getting to know God. As God speaks to you, why don't you begin to keep a spiritual journal, just for your eyes only. Write down what is taking place as you get to know God; the things the Holy Spirit is showing you; the growth in your life; your deep longings and dreams for the future. Keep a note too of your prayers and their answers. This will be very special to you as you look back.

So now you've finished your first week. You've been getting to know your Captain. Set up a time to meet your 'helper', share what's been happening, any questions you might have, and pray for each other.

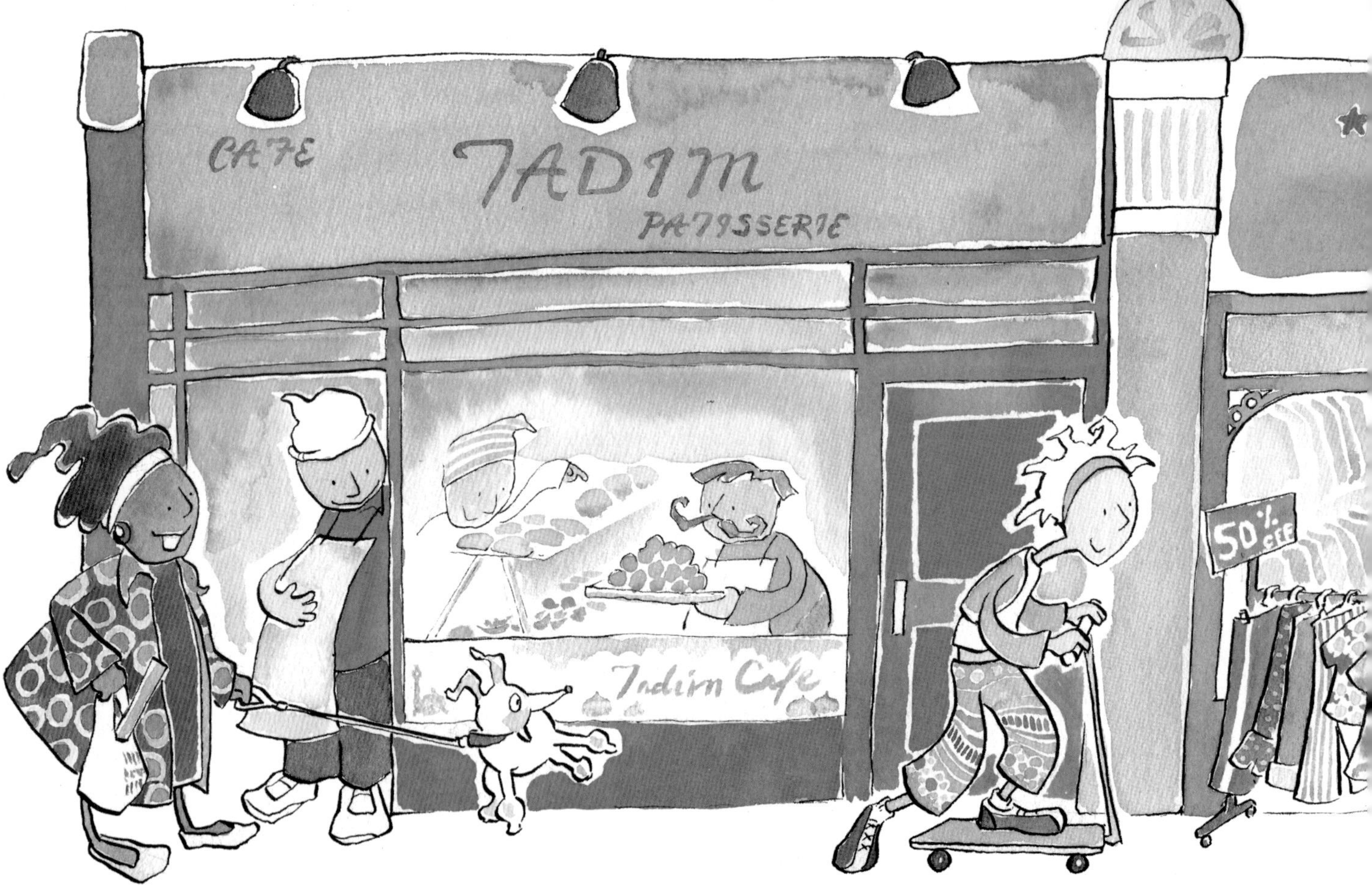
CAFE
TADIM
PATISSERIE
Tadim Cafe
50% OFF

week 2
Freedom in Jesus

day 1: Freedom from Guilt

day 2: Strongholds in Your Life

day 3: Sleeping with the Enemy

day 4: Demolishing Strongholds

day 5: The Uniform of the Kingdom

week 2
Freedom in Jesus

day 1: Freedom from Guilt

In the fifth century in Ireland, the young Patrick had a vision in which he saw himself as a lifeless, useless stone, stuck in the mud. Then something happened: 'He that is Mighty,' he wrote, ' took hold of me, and set me on top of the wall'. He could have been describing King David's experience:

> He lifted me out of the slimy pit, out of the mud and mire; he set my feet on a rock and gave me a firm place to stand.
> (Psalms 40:2)

If God were to play a video of your life until now, your actions, thoughts, motives, omissions, you might well feel very ashamed, exposed and humiliated, as if you had been in a pretty slimy and miry pit. But Jesus took all your sin and shame into himself on the cross. It took his death to deal with how bad that sin actually was in the Father's sight. That's what Jesus did for you.

What kind of feelings do you have just now?

REPENTANCE AND FORGIVENESS

Satan wants to accuse you continually before God about what you have done. He whispers to you, reminding you of your past sin. Do you experience that? Here are some promises you should take hold of by faith:

> If we confess our sins, he is faithful and just and will forgive us our sins and purify us from all unrighteousness. (1 John 1:9)

Confession is *agreeing with God about our sin*, not excusing ourselves or making light of what we have done. King David committed adultery and even murder. He cried out to God:

> Against you, you only, have I sinned and done what is evil in your sight, so that you are proved right when you speak and justified when you judge. (Psalms 51:4)

day 1 Freedom from Guilt

There are two kinds of sorrow we might have about sins we have committed. Read this, then write down what they are and what you think the difference might be:

Godly sorrow brings repentance that leads to salvation and leaves no regret, but worldly sorrow brings death. (2 Corinthians 7:10)

When we turn to God, confessing our sins, he freely forgives us, because the punishment for that sin has already been taken by Jesus on the cross. He remembers our sin no more. Someone has said, 'God has hidden our sins in the deepest sea, and put up a sign saying *No Fishing*!'

Isn't it really something that everything you have ever done wrong is forgiven by God? Sinning again mars your fellowship with Father and may allow your enemy a foothold in your life from which to harass you. Make sure you keep 'short accounts' with God. If you've sinned, tell him so, put right what you've done wrong, and ask him to restore you and to fill you again with the Holy Spirit.

SAYING SORRY

Sometimes the wrongs you have done have involved others in some way; perhaps you have hurt or cheated another person. It may be that the Spirit will lead you to ask for forgiveness, or to restore that persons reputation or property. You need wisdom for God's way and God's timing. And remember, you may say sorry, but you do not have the right to demand forgiveness. You may have to ask the Lord to give you grace to live with the consequences of some things that can never be put right. When Jesus sets you free, you're really free (Jn 8:36). If Satan accuses a forgiven sinner, God by his grace says, 'I don't remember that sin.' Remember, although grace is *free*, it wasn't *cheap*. Freedom from guilt cost Jesus' death for you on the cross.

Today, spend some time with Father thanking him for what he has done in forgiving your deepest sins and giving you freedom in Jesus. Perhaps you should make a private entry in your journal. Ask him to test your heart. Is the Lord leading you to any particular action? Psalm 51 might be helpful.

Finally, your memory verse for this week:

If we confess our sins, he is faithful and just and will forgive us our sins and purify us from all unrighteousness. (1 John 1:9)

week 2
Freedom in Jesus

day 2: Strongholds in Your Life

Even though you may sincerely desire to follow Jesus and you have been given a *'new spirit'* (Ezekiel 36:26), there may be in your physical and emotional make-up long-standing habits and ideas, deep hurts or rejection that still need the healing touch of Jesus. There may even be areas in which you still find yourself resisting the claims of Jesus on your life. The Bible calls areas of our mind that resist God for any reason *'strongholds'*.

Strongholds also exist in the minds of those who are not Christians, in families, city populations, or in whole nations. These may be any kind of false beliefs or attitudes, hatred of other people groups, extreme nationalism, counterfeit forms of Christianity, idolatry and worldly value systems.

We are called upon to engage in a form of battle against these strongholds, revealing instead the values of the Kingdom of God. But it is not an ordinary fight. It is not won by human means; it is a battle that takes place in the spiritual realm. The strongholds are in the mind; the enemy is not people, but spiritual beings and their strategies; the weapons are prayer and the authority of Jesus.

Paul writes about strongholds in 2 Corinthians 10, verses 3 – 5:

> *For though we live in the world, we do not wage war as the world does. The weapons we fight with are not the weapons of the world. On the contrary, they have divine power to demolish strongholds. We demolish arguments and every pretension that sets itself up against the knowledge of God, and we take captive every thought to make it obedient to Christ.*

Can you see from this passage what *Satan's intended purpose* for strongholds is?

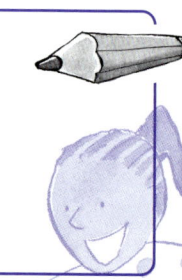

To help you recognise what kinds of behaviour or experiences might lead to strongholds, let's put some names on these dark fortresses. Some are things you've done or are doing; some result from the pain of bad experiences and from which you might need healing. In some you will be able to move into victory alone; in others you may need the counsel and prayer ministry of one of your leaders or someone who focuses on helping others break free.

NAMING SOME STRONGHOLDS

- Bitterness towards someone who has hurt you.
- Resentment, grudges, unwillingness to forgive.
- Fears and shame resulting from abuse.
- Occult practices (ouija board, tarot, horoscopes – see Leviticus 20:6–8; Deuteronomy 17:1–5).
- Extreme nationalism; hatred of other peoples.
- Addictions (to substances, gambling, TV).
- Gluttony, overeating.
- Pornography (Job 31:1).
- Hostility, jealousy, gossip.
- Controlling, manipulative behaviour.
- Role-playing fantasies.
- Immoral relationships; homosexual practice. (Ephesians 5:3; Leviticus 18:22; Romans 1:26,27).
- Health-destroying habits.
- Inferiority complex hindering your freedom.
- Effects of rejection (Isaiah 49:15,16).
- Patterns of sin in parents and grandparents.
- 'Doctrines of demons' (1 Timothy 4:1).

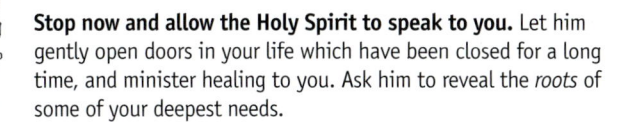

Stop now and allow the Holy Spirit to speak to you. Let him gently open doors in your life which have been closed for a long time, and minister healing to you. Ask him to reveal the *roots* of some of your deepest needs.

EXPOSING THE LIE

Satan's language is lying (another stronghold), and we need to confront him with truth. Jesus said of Satan:

> *He was a murderer from the beginning, not holding to the truth, for there is no truth in him. When he lies, he speaks his native language, for he is a liar and the father of lies. (John 8:44)*

So **Step 1** in the spiritual battle is to **equip your mind with truth**. When you expose a lie of Satan, make a declaration of truth by faith, e.g. 'Satan, you are a thief. You have nothing to offer me. Jesus has everything I need.' As you learn the Word of God you will be better equipped to recognise the lie.

Step 2 is to **take every thought captive and submit it to Jesus in prayer**. Any double-mindedness will fade away as the peace of God guards your heart and mind. (Philippians 4:7)

Step 3 is to **replace the works of the devil with Father's works.** Living in the Spirit means that Jesus' kingdom values replace those of the world.

Make a note of any questions raised by reading the list of strongholds that you would like to ask your helper.

week 2
Freedom in Jesus

day 3: Sleeping with the Enemy

IDENTIFYING THE ENEMY

Every follower of Jesus knows that living by the values of the Kingdom involves a battle. And hostile fire comes from three sources: **the world around us, the desires within us**, **and the devil.** Have a look at this passage in 1 John 2:15–17. Turn it up in your own Bible and underline it:

> *Do not love the world or anything in the world. If anyone loves the world, the love of the Father is not in him. For everything in the world – the cravings of sinful man, the lust of his eyes and the boasting of what he has and does – comes not from the Father but from the world. The world and its desires pass away, but the man who does the will of God lives for ever.*

What does John mean by 'the world and its desires'?

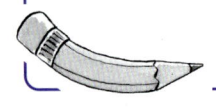

Now turn up this passage in Ephesians 6:12:

> *For our struggle is not against flesh and blood, but against the rulers, against the authorities, against the powers of this dark world and against the spiritual forces of evil in the heavenly realms.*

Paul says that our enemies are not people at all; they are spirits – demonic powers of various kinds. It appears that these powers are angels that rebelled against God. They are agents for 'the thief' who seek to steal and destroy anything that reflects the image of God in us. You have power from the Holy Spirit to defeat these enemies in your own life, and, as you grow, to minister freedom to others. Remember what Jesus' mission was? (Hint – Acts 10:38).

VICTORY

Let's look at how spirit powers operate. When Jesus was nailed to the cross, Satan must have been dancing with delight. It was as though he was taunting the Lord with a list of your sins, saying, 'this one is mine; he rejected you when he sinned.' But Jesus, as it were, grabbed the list of your sins and it was nailed to the cross with him. He set you free by paying the price for what you had done – the wages of sin is death. He then burst out of the tomb and defeated not only sin, but death itself, the consequence of sin.
Read Colossians 2:13–15. Then shout Hallelujah!

Jesus has defeated the powers and set you free! When you came to him in repentance and faith, he transferred you, as with every believer, from . . .

> the dominion of darkness and brought us into the kingdom of the Son he loves, in whom we have redemption, the forgiveness of sins. (Colossians 1:13,14)

SLEEPING WITH THE ENEMY

So how then do spirit powers continue to have the ability to establish strongholds? **Sin is like an illicit liaison with the enemy whereby we are unfaithful to God**. Its offspring is destruction. When we sin repeatedly Satan is legally given a 'foothold' in our lives (see Ephesians 4:27). Repentance takes away this foothold.

Allow the Holy Spirit to search your heart as you read this section on footholds. Let's look at some again:

1. Occult practices. If you have sought protection or guidance from *any* power other than Jesus, you have opened yourself up to *occultism*. Do you have lucky charms to protect you, medals or medallions; have you consulted a fortune teller (medium) or used a ouija board; have you attempted to contact the dead; chanted a mantra; talked with a spirit guide; regularly read horoscopes, tea leaves or tarot cards? Are you superstitious?

If so, you may have been involved in *witchcraft* or *spiritism*. God is our only Protector and Provider. Even 'innocent' practices like 'touching wood' or 'crossing your fingers' are forms of lucky charms. Depending on 'saints' or spirit guides must be totally rejected, for

> there is one God and one mediator between God and men, the man Christ Jesus. (1 Timothy 2:5)

As Peter said,

> Salvation is found in no one else, for there is no other name under heaven given to men by which we must be saved.' (Acts 4:12)

2. Sin. As we noted earlier, habitual patterns of sin, in words, actions or attitudes, may allow a stronghold to develop.

3. Resentment. Deep hurts caused by others may continue to allow the enemy to hurt you further if bitterness and resentment remain unhealed as a result of withholding forgiveness.

Spend time today thanking Father that everything you need is in him. Allow this truth to set you free of trying to find life anywhere else. Oh, and don't forget to review your two memory verses.

week 2
Freedom in Jesus

day 4: Demolishing Strongholds

Demolishing a stronghold means that Satan no longer has that base in your life from which to harass you and hinder your growth. As the fortresses are eliminated, more and more of the Kingdom of God is coming in. Ed Silvoso suggests that if Heaven has a daily paper (The Morning Star?!) one wonderful day it will probably carry a headline something like this:

> THEY OVERCAME SATAN
> by the blood of the Lamb and by the word of their testimony; they did not love their lives so much as to shrink from death.
> (Revelation 12:11)

THE OVERCOMERS

Do you want to be an overcomer? Jesus has already defeated Satan by the cross, and his victory is yours. So set aside some time now to pray and to let God speak to you. Try to arrange it so that there are no interruptions. Whether you are alone or have sought out someone to help you as you claim freedom in Jesus, **follow these steps at your own pace**:

(On Day 2 this week we mentioned some steps in pulling down strongholds. Let's develop them a little further so you can pray through them.)

1. DECLARE THE TRUTH. Pray something like this, or use your own words:

> *Father, everything I need is in you. Everything you do is good. I praise you and thank you that the Lord Jesus paid in full for my sin and rose again to give me new life. He is exalted above every power, and all authority on the earth and in the heavens belongs to him. Father, you have given me new birth to live in your kingdom, and I am your child. I claim by faith now the victory of the Lord Jesus and ask your Holy Spirit's protection as I battle with the enemy.*

Helpful Scriptures include Ephesians 3:14–19; Psalm 27; Psalm 119:25–32.

2. SUBMIT YOURSELF TO GOD, RESIST THE DEVIL. Bring every thought before him and submit it to the light of his way:

> *Father, I submit all my thoughts to you now. I bring all my hopes and dreams, my fears, all my needs, and I lay them at your feet. I ask instead for your plans for me. Lord Jesus, send your Holy Spirit now to witness with my spirit. Lord, I thank you that in you I have power to demolish these strongholds in my life . . . [say them by name to the Lord]. I confess my sin before you.*

day 4 Demolishing Strongholds

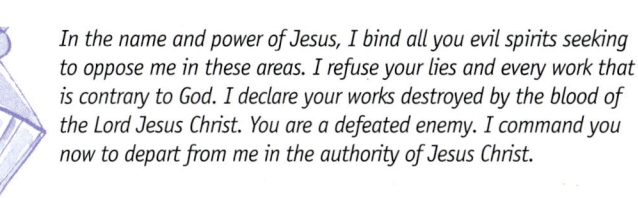

In the name and power of Jesus, I bind all you evil spirits seeking to oppose me in these areas. I refuse your lies and every work that is contrary to God. I declare your works destroyed by the blood of the Lord Jesus Christ. You are a defeated enemy. I command you now to depart from me in the authority of Jesus Christ.

Helpful Scriptures: James 3:14–16 and 4:7–10; 1 Peter 5: 6–10.

3. BE FILLED WITH THE HOLY SPIRIT. Jesus said that it was dangerous to drive a spirit out of a house and then just leave it empty; other worse ones would return (see Luke 11:24–26). Driving out *evil* spirits must be followed by the filling of the *Holy* Spirit and the works of the kingdom of God.

We'll introduce you more fully to the 'baptism in the Holy Spirit' in *Making Headway*, but for now here's a prayer for the Holy Spirit to fill you. Then we'll see how the Father's works might flow in to replace those of the enemy. The works of the devil are a *stench* in God's nostrils; the Holy Spirit brings the new *fragrance* of the presence, character and actions of the Lord Jesus.

Holy Spirit, I ask you now to come and fill every part of my being – my mind, my will, my emotions. I ask for a fresh empowering in my life, so that Jesus' life will flow in me and through me. Transform my mind, so that I think the thoughts of the Father. Fill my heart with a longing to do his will. Give me power to confront the evil one and to destroy his works. Replace the values of the world in my life with the values of the Kingdom of the Heavens, in Jesus' lovely name. Amen.

EARTHWORKS

Finally today, consider how the 'upside-down kingdom' of the Lord Jesus turns the world 'right side up' when God's will is done on *earth* as it is in *heaven*. Where a stronghold has existed, ask the Lord to show you what the opposite Kingdom spirit is to that which has entrapped you. In the world there is a *selfish* spirit; in the Kingdom a *servant* spirit. In the world *rejection*; in the Kingdom *acceptance*. In the world a spirit of *lying*; in the Kingdom a spirit of *truth*. In the world *reputation* and *image* are everything; in the Kingdom the *character of Jesus* is most important.

Is there a 'Kingdom action' which the Lord is leading you to take to reverse the spirit of the strongholds which he has broken, and when should you do it?

Action _____

Time _____

week 2
Freedom in Jesus

day 5: The Uniform of the Kingdom

THE POLICEMAN IN THE BROWN SUIT*

So here you are driving along the road one day, and this man in a brown suit stands out in front of you, raises his hand and says 'halt'. And as you get close you say 'Ah that's only John Smith who lives around the corner. I know him. His wife's name is Betty and he has six kids.' And you decide not to bother stopping.

The next day there's the same man whom you thought you knew, but now he's in a police uniform, with shiny silver buttons, and a white car with a blue stripe and blue flashing lights, and a police STOP sign in red. It isn't just 'John Smith' that's holding up his hand now. Behind him is the head of the whole Police Force; and behind him is the Lord Chief Justice; and behind him is the prison!

So weighing everything up in a flash, you decide you'd better stop! What was it on the second day that changed your mind? *It was the authority of the blue uniform.*

THE UNIFORM OF THE KINGDOM

If you were to try to command the enemy to stop his wicked work in your own strength and natural identity, he would pay no attention to you. You might get 'beaten up'. But as a member of God's army you *do* have a uniform. The authority behind that uniform is not just you, but the hosts of heaven, and their Commander in Chief, the Lord Jesus Christ, and the lake of fire reserved for the devil and his angels. You have *Kingdom* authority.

Paul describes the uniform in Ephesians 6:13–18. *Stop now and read this passage, then list on the left the parts of the uniform and on the right what you think they stand for.*

---

* This is a development of an illustration I first came across in one of Dr James Dobson's *Focus on the Family* film series.

day 5 | The Uniform of the Kingdom

THE UNIFORM IS JESUS HIMSELF

You might think that Paul got his idea from a Roman soldier. But no, it was an Old Testament description of God himself from Isaiah 59. God was appalled that there was no one to intercede for the people who were crushed by their oppressors. Everywhere he looked there was rebellion, unrighteousness and dishonesty.

So it says of him (v 17):

> He put on righteousness as his breastplate, and the helmet of salvation on his head; he put on the garments of vengeance and wrapped himself in zeal as in a cloak.

It was a picture of God jumping out of heaven dressed in armour which was his own character – that is, salvation, righteousness and judgment. When the Lord Jesus came to earth, he brought salvation and righteousness and judgment on the enemy and on sin. He was, in that sense, a warrior.

You are also a soldier of the Kingdom. But the armour you put on is *Jesus himself*. In him you have *truth, salvation, righteousness, peace, faith,* and, by the Holy Spirit, *the Word,* or breath of God in your mouth as a sword with which to slay the enemy!

But the instruction is to *put on* the armour.

PUTTING ON YOUR UNIFORM

In order to be a well-dressed Christian soldier, you need to put on your uniform *by faith*. As you close this very important week, go to your quiet place and, piece by piece, put on your armour before the Lord. Say something like this:

> *In your presence, Lord, I take the helmet of salvation. I praise you with great joy that salvation belongs to you and that you have saved me from my enemy and from my sin. By faith I put on Christ today, who is my life and my salvation. My authority comes from you, O Lord. I am saved! I am saved!*

As you learn to *pray Scripture,* ask the Holy Spirit to bring to your mind the significance of each piece of the uniform. Talk with your helper this weekend, and pray like this together.

Our focus this week has been *Freedom in Jesus.* Look back over the week at what God has been doing in your life to bring you into new areas of freedom. Remember, this is only the beginning; the Father will gently lead you through many such learning times in the wonderful years ahead.

You should by now know two memory passages by heart.

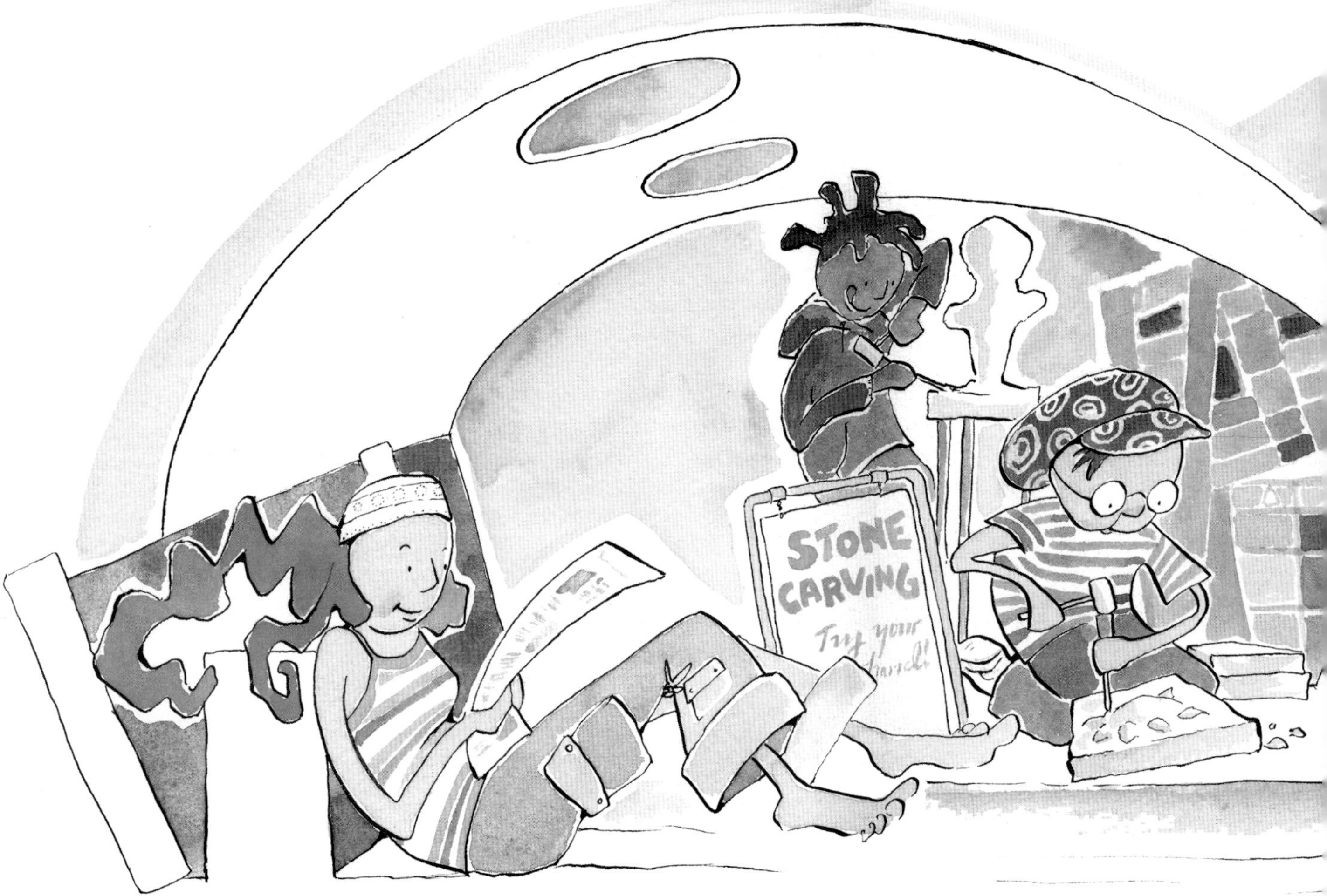
STONE CARVING
Try your hand!

week 3
The Kingdom of God

day 1: The Jesus Manifesto

day 2: The Prescence of the Future

day 3: Mission Impossible

day 4: The Community of the King

day 5: Your Kingdom Birthright

week 3
The Kingdom of God

day 1: The Jesus Manifesto

At the time these notes are being written there is a clever series of ads in which the world looks wildly different when viewed through a Smirnoff bottle. Sometimes a movement begins that entirely changes the way people see reality; it becomes a new *world view*. The new message has to be explained in a *manifesto* of some kind, in such a way as to capture the imagination and commitment of the new generation.

The *Communist Manifesto* was published in 1847, eventually changing the values of whole countries. In 1933 the *Humanist Manifesto* claimed that there was no higher authority than *man* to give us values.

Jesus too had a message, a manifesto, that reversed the world's values and turned the world 'upside down'. His message leads to a future fulfilment so utterly amazing, so *earth-shattering* in its impact and implications, that the most wonder-filled fairy tale seems dull in comparison. Paul saw it like this in 1 Corinthians 2:9:

No eye has seen, no ear has heard, no mind has conceived what God has prepared for those who love him.

If someone were to ask you whether things look different to you now that you've become a Christian, what would you tell them? (Acts 26:15–18 is an *eye opener*!)

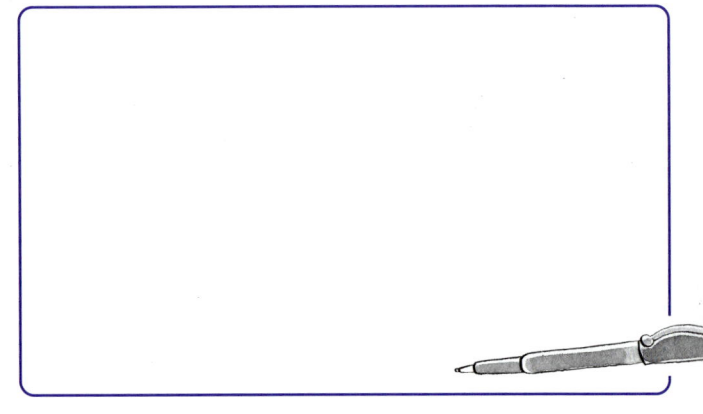

JESUS' EYE-OPENING MESSAGE

As you begin to understand Jesus' amazing message, your heart will be captivated more and more by a new way of looking at the world, its people, its history, its values, its sorrows and vain hopes, and its future. So, let's begin to have a look at Jesus' message; as you follow him you're going to be sharing this with others in various ways.

day 1   The Jesus Manifesto

Jesus began his ministry with a truly dramatic announcement:

> 'The time has come,' he said. 'The kingdom of God is near. Repent and believe the good news!' (Mark 1:15)

It was dramatic because t*he people had longed for this moment for centuries*. They had yearned for a time when God would reign as King. Dozens of prophecies had told about the One who would come as Deliverer, Saviour, King, the Prince of Peace whose Kingdom would have no end, and who would bring in justice and righteousness for ever. (If you have time today you may read some of these prophecies in Isaiah 9:6–8; 61:1–3; Daniel 2:44; Zechariah 9:9). And now Jesus was saying 'It's time!'

It was dramatic because *the King Himself was present*. In Jesus, the Kingdom reign of God was at their very fingertips. If anyone wants to be part of God's Kingdom, to grab handfuls of it and take it into their lives, all they have to do is reach out and take hold of Jesus the King. In him the Kingdom is near. (Remember God 'jumping out of heaven' when we looked at the Uniform of the Kingdom?)

And Jesus' announcement was dramatic because it was *a call to a total change of direction for one's life*. Repentance means just that – a decision that involves a turning back from sin and from the world's values. Although repentance often involves deep sorrow or tears, it is not so much an emotion as an *action* – an *act of faith*. It also means *a change of mind about Jesus*. The call to repentance was a call to make a personal commitment to him. *Let the Spirit touch you now, strengthening this work of repentance in your heart, helping you see the world through the lens of God's Kingdom.*

THE JESUS MANIFESTO

Jesus both *explained* his Kingdom and *demonstrated* it. Much of his Kingdom *teaching* is in 'The Sermon on the Mount' found in Matthew's gospel, chapters 5 to 7. *It is to do with what it is like when the Father's will is done on earth as it is in heaven, and the works of the devil are being destroyed.* It teaches the 'upside-down' values of the Kingdom in opposition to the world's values. Jesus taught that *counterfeit religion* values such things as pomp, titles, self-glorifying 'charity', prayers babbled like pagans; the Kingdom is about relationship and intimacy with the Father, serving others, loving and forgiving enemies, always speaking the truth; it's about financial honesty, a new view of 'treasure', faithfulness and purity in sexual matters (see 1 Thess 4:1–8), life that survives catastrophe because it is built on a solid 'rock'.

Today in your quiet place ask the Holy Spirit to speak to you about Kingdom values. He expresses them in you as you allow Jesus' life to flow through you. Remember, just act supernaturally! Read some of Matthew chapter 5.

Finally, this week's (easy!) memory verse:

> *But seek first his kingdom and his righteousness, and all these things will be given to you as well. (Matthew 6:33)*

week 3
The Kingdom of God

day 2: The Presence of the Future

One day you will hear three amazing sounds that will shake the whole earth! Look in your Bible now and read about them in 1 Thessalonians 4:16–18. What are they, and what's happening? How do you feel about this?

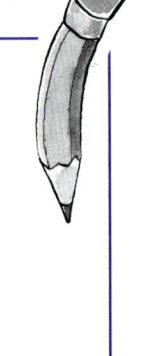

THE RETURN OF JESUS CHRIST

Jesus is coming again in power and great glory, to establish the fullness of his Kingdom on the earth. This is the climax towards which all history is moving. At this time (and in the times following), some unimaginable and wondrous things will happen in the universe which are spoken about throughout the scriptures:

- Jesus will *take authority over all nations of the earth*; all human government will be suspended. The rulers of the earth will give account to Jesus. (Matthew 25:31,32)
- The antichrist ruler will be *destroyed* along with the world's false religious leader. (Revelation 19:19,20)
- All faithful followers of Jesus who have died and all who are still alive will receive a *new body* in which they will live for ever. (Philippians 3:20,21; 1 Corinthians 15:51–53)
- Government of the earth will be given *to believers*. (Revelation 5:9,10)
- There will be *no more death*. (Revelation 21:4)
- There will be *no more mourning, crying or pain*.
- The physical creation will be *set free* from the results of humanity's sin. (Romans 8:19–23)
- Everything will be *made new*. (Revelation 21:5)
- Every person on earth will *see Jesus*. (Revelation 1:7)
- Satan and his demons will eventually be *cast into the lake of fire*. (Revelation 20:10)
- Everyone who followed Satan will be *excluded from God's Kingdom*. (1 Corinthians 6:9,10)
- A new eternal *age of righteousness and peace will begin,* with the Lord himself reigning in all his beauty and glory, worshipped for ever and ever by people from every nation, and by the angels. (Revelation 7:9–12; 11:15)

day 2 — The Presence of the Future

How did you feel as you read these passages? Record some things that were new discoveries, or any questions you have.

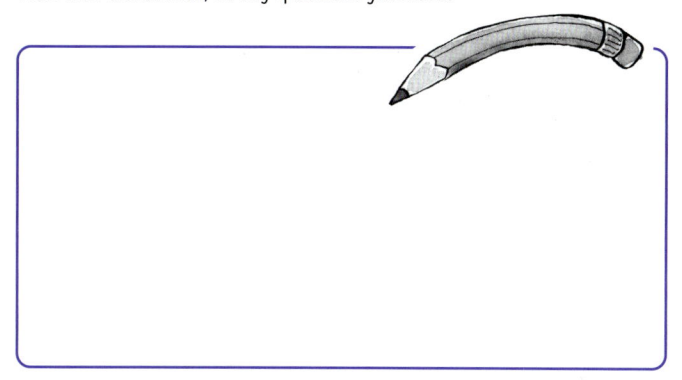

ALREADY AND NOT YET

These are amazing truths about what it will be like when the works of the devil have been destroyed fully, and the Kingdom comes. But didn't Jesus say that the Kingdom was here already?

To understand this paradox, let's first look at what Jesus was actually doing – his *ministry*. In Matthew 4:23–25 Jesus preached and *demonstrated* the Kingdom. He healed every disease and sickness, including severe pain, epilepsy and paralysis, and he cast out demons. He even raised the dead. Doesn't it sound like something of the future was breaking into the present?

As Jesus was demonstrating the Kingdom, something of heaven was coming to earth. Father's will was being done.

Yet the battle continues. Nations and individuals still rebel against God. There are still spiritual enemies. People still get sick and die. Evil will remain until Jesus comes. The fullness of the Kingdom is *not yet*. But in the meantime, in the power of the Holy Spirit, something of the future new age of the Kingdom breaks into the present. It's like this:

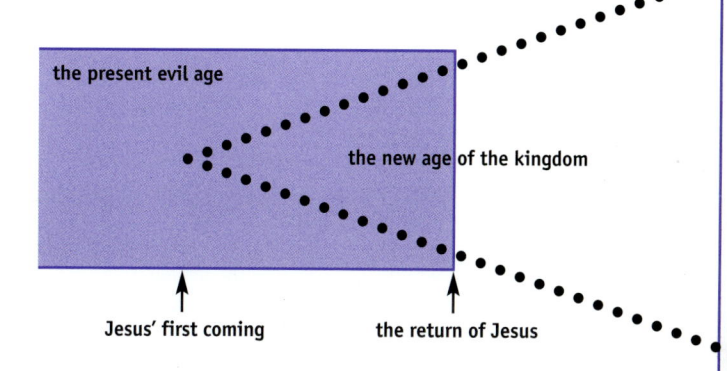

the present evil age

the new age of the kingdom

↑ Jesus' first coming   ↑ the return of Jesus

We are living in the *overlap of the ages,* a time in which Jesus wants you to continue the works he began (John 14:12). As you follow him in the power of the Holy Spirit, you too will experience something of the *already* of the Kingdom of God, and see the devil's works destroyed.

week 3
The Kingdom of God

day 3: Mission Impossible

Already, the Holy Spirit has been equipping you to be part of a mission which, in your natural abilities, is *totally impossible*! He is preparing you to bring the Kingdom of Heaven into the lives of others, just as Jesus did. It has little, in one way, to do with who you are or what your story has been; it has everything to do with who *Jesus is in you*. Read Matthew 19:26:

> Jesus looked at them and said, 'With man this is impossible, but with God all things are possible.'

It's not just that all things are possible *for* God, but that since his Holy Spirit is in us, all things are possible *with* him.

In another way, it does have to do with who you are, for you have been fashioned with great care by God, ideally crafted for the Kingdom ministry he has saved you for.

> *For we are God's workmanship, created in Christ Jesus to do good works, which God prepared in advance for us to do.*
> *(Ephesians 2:10)*

DREAM THE IMPOSSIBLE DREAM

Let's do a little dreaming today. Jesus said that if you asked for anything in his name he would do it (John 14:12–14). Instead of trying to limit or qualify that invitation, let's ask for things so big that only God could do them. So, if Jesus were to ask you now, '[Your name], how would you like me to use you in my Kingdom?', what would you say? Look at the list below and mark off your desire.

- [ ] To lay hands on people and see them healed
- [ ] To have the gift of prophecy
- [ ] To be able to teach the Scriptures
- [ ] To lead hundreds of others to Jesus
- [ ] To pray for impossible situations in my area and see God answer (such as _____)
- [ ] To bring Jesus' love to hurting people
- [ ] To lead others into worship in Spirit and truth
- [ ] To bring financial support to kingdom work
- [ ] To study theology, or train for leadership
- [ ] To stand for justice and against oppression
- [ ] To set people free from demonic oppression
- [ ] To use practical skills to advance the Kingdom
- [ ] To represent Jesus on TV, or in print media

day 3 | Mission Impossible

Write down how you would like God to use you. God's wisdom will guide you and guard you if you ask for something foolish. But don't be afraid to ask; let your faith be in the bigness of God. Dream impossible dreams.

God has used many people whose stories will never be known until Jesus comes. With others, the seeds sown didn't sprout until they had died. Yet God was pleased with them. He just wants those who are available to be used in his Kingdom service.

Jackie Pullinger left England for Hong Kong in her early twenties. Helpless and without experience, God used her to bring the power of the Kingdom to the triad gangs that controlled the criminal underworld in the area known as *The Walled City*. You can read her story in her book *Chasing the Dragon*.

You don't need to try to *copy* what the Holy Spirit has done in someone else's life. But he can use you right where you live, to bring his Kingdom to everyone you meet. Just tell him now that you'd like that.

When you meet with your helper later this week, perhaps you could pray together about some of your dreams. Don't worry if they're not too clear yet.

Was today encouraging, or scary?
The 'heavenly realms' are a pretty dramatic place to live, all right!

Finally, review your memory verse from Matthew 6:33.

week 3
The Kingdom of God

day 4: The Community of the King

When you were *born again of the Father* you became part of his family. Since every true believer has the Father's life in them, they are in reality your brothers and sisters. It is by meeting this family that the world sees the kingdom of God through a loving, healing, restoring, upbuilding community. God's family is the *Community of the King*. It is called *the Church*.

What images or ideas come to your mind when you think of 'church'? Do you feel positively or negatively about 'church'?

Perhaps you thought of church as a *building* – a church. In the Bible the word *church* never, ever refers to a building. In fact, the believers used to meet in small groups in houses, just as your cell group is doing. In Romans 16:3–5 Paul sends greetings to some friends, and 'the church that meets at their house'. You may even have thought of church as a *meeting*, as in, 'I'll meet you after church'. Again, although in the Bible churches *met*, the meeting was not itself *church*. In fact, when the meeting was over, the church went out the front door!

Maybe you thought of the church as the *clergy*. We might speak of 'going into the church', meaning becoming a priest or a clergyman (or woman!). Again, the word *church* is never used in this way in the Bible. (In fact, *no Christian leader is ever called a priest in the New Testament*.) Church in Scripture doesn't refer to the leaders.

Finally, you may have thought of church as a particular *denomination or organisation,* e.g. the Catholic Church, the Church of Scotland, the Church of England. Many within these organisations have a true relationship with Jesus. When the Bible speaks of *the church,* however, it means *all people called out from the world to follow Jesus Christ*. These are the people of the Kingdom; and you have become a citizen of this Kingdom. Christians meeting locally are called *churches* (see Romans 16:16). Your cell group is part of a local church.

So let's see if we can recover the beauty and excitement of the church as seen in the Scriptures. Several word pictures will help us understand.

day 4 The Community of the King

THE BRIDE (Matthew 25:1–13)

One of the loveliest pictures is that of a *bride*. Jesus loves his bride, the church. They are the people the Father has won for his Son. When Jesus returns, there will be a great wedding feast as the bride is united with her Beloved, the Lord Jesus Christ.

THE FAMILY (1 John 3:1)

We have already seen how, since God is our Father, all true Christians are our family. What kind of words do you associate with a good family? (Dangerous question!)

THE BODY (Ephesians 4:16; 1 Corinthians 12)

The Scriptures also picture the church as a body in which each part has a special purpose. And yet every part depends on others for the body to function. Jesus is the Head of the body. No one on earth is 'head of the church'.

THE ARMY OF GOD (2 Timothy 2:3)

An army exists to defeat enemies and enforce or extend the rule of a king. The church is like an army too, but instead of being destructive of *people*, its enemies are spiritual powers and their schemes. It is a redemptive army, waging war with weapons of love, hope, kindness and healing.

TEAMWORK

Remember our little boat? Your cell group is like a little crew in a *fellowship – a basic Christian community,* modelling the Kingdom to everyone by loving one another with Jesus' love. They are also training together for Kingdom ministry and mission. God has given *leaders* to nurture and equip you and to steer the ship. Your cell is part of a larger 'fleet', your local church. And that is itself a part of the whole church of Jesus in Britain and the world.

There's so much more to learn about the advance of Jesus' church. Just remember this: It's his church, *he loves it,* and *it will never fail.* And you're just *beginning* the adventure!

Spend some time today praying for each person in your cell group, for your helper, your cell leader and assistant leader, and for other leaders in the Fellowship. Let them know you are praying for their ministry, their families, and for their protection from the works of the enemy.

week 3
The Kingdom of God

day 5: Your Kingdom Birthright

BORN TWICE IN THE SAME HOUSE

I was born twice in the same house. Really. The first time I was born as a child of my parents; the second time, 17 years later, I was born again as a child of God. The first time – because Adam opened a door into the world for Satan – I was born into a sin-damaged world, and following its ways, I became a *sinner*. But when I was born the second time, it was of the Holy Spirit; I became a *saint*.

The day you were born again you became a saint too. *Saint* means 'holy, set apart from evil, sanctified'. *Every Christian is a saint*. There are no 'special' people called *Saint* anything. Peter was just 'Peter', not Saint Peter, though like you, he was a saint. God *set you apart* for himself when he gave you life by the *Holy* Spirit. You're a whole new person.

> *Therefore, if anyone is in Christ, he is a new creation; the old has gone, the new has come! (2 Corinthians 5:17)*

Satan tries to deceive you about who you are, wanting to make you live *out of your old life*. As a child of God you have power to live life in a completely different way, because you are called to live *out of your new life*. Sometimes we listen to the wrong voice, make the wrong choices, do 'Adam' things. Even saints can sin. But your essential identity is no longer in *Adam*, a sinner; you are in *Christ*, a saint. If you do sin, confess it, turn from it, and receive the Father's forgiveness. You are still his child.

Is this making sense? *Who you are* determines *how you live*. It is stupid to live as if you were someone else. Sinning is living as if you were someone else – a child of Adam. Now that you're *in Christ*, what's true of him is true of you.

So today, let's look at *who you are*. Read this list out loud every time the enemy tries to tell you you're a nobody, that God doesn't care about you, or that you'll never amount to anything.

In fact, why don't you do that right now. In your quiet place make these 'Kingdom birthright' declarations by faith. Come back to this page when you face an 'identity crisis'. You'll be glad you did.

day 5 Your Kingdom Birthright

THE REAL ME

- I am a child of God; he is my Father. (Romans 8:16; Galatians 3:26; 1 John 3:1)

- I am an heir of the Father's inheritance in Jesus. (Romans 8:17; Galatians 3:29; 1 Peter 1:4)

- I am a saint of the Most High God. (Philippians 1:1)

- I am a new creation in Christ. (2 Corinthians 5:17)

- I am a temple where God lives by his Spirit. (1 Corinthians 3:16)

- I am a friend of Jesus Christ. (John 15:15)

- I belong to the people of God, chosen to be a royal priesthood and a holy nation. (1 Peter 2:9)

- The full payment for my sin has been paid at the cross, and my debt is cancelled. (Colossians 1:14)

- I have everything I need for life and godliness. (2 Peter 1:3)

- I have been bought with a price: I belong to God. (1 Corinthians 6:19,20)

- I am a fellow citizen of God's Kingdom with all true Christians everywhere. (Ephesians 2:19)

- I have been rescued from the dominion of darkness and brought into the Kingdom of the Son God loves. (Colossians 1:13)

- Since I am in Christ, I am chosen for his purposes and I am holy and dearly loved. (Colossians 3:12)

- I am an enemy of the devil (don't be afraid to declare it.) (1 Peter 5:8)

- I am a minister of reconciliation. (2 Corinthians 5:18,19)

- I am the light of the world (just as Jesus is.) (Matthew 5:14)

- I am the very righteousness of God. (2 Corinthians 5:21)

- Through God's promises I partake in the divine nature. (2 Peter 1:4)

- I myself may approach God's throne with boldness for mercy and grace in time of need. (Hebrews 4:16)

There are so many more truths you may discover about your true identity, 'the real you'. When you do, write them in your spiritual journal.

Finally, review your memory verse for this week.

MARKET

HAIR PRODUCTS
TEXTILES
CDs

SALE

week 4
The Word of God

- day 1: God's Powerful Word
- day 2: Modern Versions
- day 3: Reading the Bible for Yourself
- day 4: Spending an Hour in Prayer
- day 5: The Way Ahead

week 4
The Word of God

day 1: God's Powerful Word

This week we are going to concentrate on the Bible itself. It is God's revelation of himself and his purposes in history and eternity. The Bible is, so to speak, God's very breath; it is *inspired*. 'Inspired' doesn't mean 'brilliant!' as in, say, an inspired play or symphony. It means that *God himself has breathed the message* that is expressed in the human words of its authors. They were not just writing down their own religious ideas.

> *Above all, you must understand that no prophecy of Scripture came about by the prophet's own interpretation. For prophecy never had its origin in the will of man, but men spoke from God as they were carried along by the Holy Spirit. (2 Peter 1:20,21)*
>
> *All Scripture is God-breathed . . . (2 Timothy 3:16)*

In what way has God spoken to you through the Bible?

GOD'S WORD IS POWERFUL

Consider the following passages about what happens when God speaks, and write down what kind of power is being described:

- *And God said, 'Let there be light,' and there was light. (Genesis 1:3)*

- *For the word of God is living and active. Sharper than any double-edged sword, it penetrates even to dividing soul and spirit, joints and marrow; it judges the thoughts and attitudes of the heart. (Hebrews 4:12)*

- *How can a young man keep his way pure? By living according to your word. (Psalm 119:9)*

- *All Scripture is God-breathed and is useful for teaching, rebuking, correcting and training in righteousness. (2 Timothy 3:16)*

day 1 God's Powerful Word

- *Because our gospel came to you not simply with words, but also with power, with the Holy Spirit and with deep conviction.*
  (1 Thessalonians 1:5)

_____

- *He [Jesus] will strike the earth with the rod of his mouth; with the breath of his lips he will slay the wicked. (Isaiah 11:4)*

_____

Perhaps we could say that God's power is *creative* power, *convicting* power, *cleansing* power, *correcting* power, *converting* power, *conquering* power!

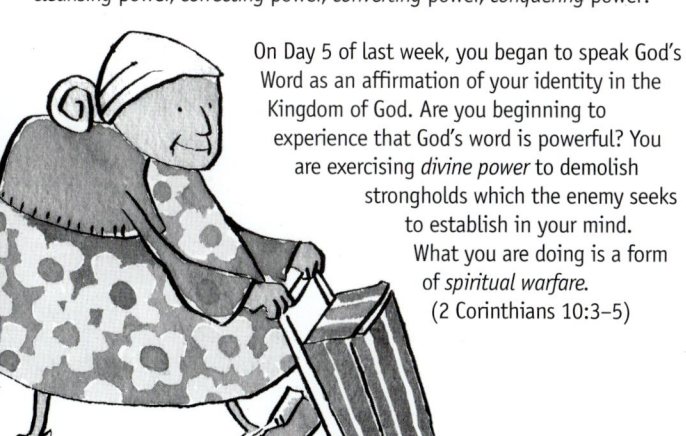

On Day 5 of last week, you began to speak God's Word as an affirmation of your identity in the Kingdom of God. Are you beginning to experience that God's word is powerful? You are exercising *divine power* to demolish strongholds which the enemy seeks to establish in your mind. What you are doing is a form of *spiritual warfare*.
(2 Corinthians 10:3–5)

GOD'S WORD IS PRECIOUS

Not only is God's Word powerful, transforming lives, it is precious. Of his words, Psalm 19:10 says:

> *They are more precious than gold, than much pure gold; they are sweeter than honey, than honey from the comb.*

And like precious stones, God's words outlast everything else:

> *Heaven and earth will pass away, but my words will never pass away. (Matthew 24:35)*

So, as you begin this Kingdom adventure, the Word of God will become precious to you; it will show you truth which will set you free; it will cast a light on your path; it will be like honey to your lips. (Mmmmm!)

Take some time now and read Psalm 19:7–11 in the presence of the Lord. Let the Lord speak to you as you do. Ask him to give you a love for his precious, powerful Word. Write in your journal anything you feel God is saying to you as you read.

Your memory verse for this final week of *Welcome Aboard* is from Hebrews 4:12, which you've already read today. It's printed on the previous page, but underline it in your Bible. It will help you for many years to come.

49

week 4
The Word of God

day 2: Modern Versions

Open up the title page of your Bible, and see which *translation* it is. We are privileged to have, in the English language, the greatest number of modern translations. At first this will seem a bit confusing, but it is a very positive thing as we'll see in a momemt. Tick off any translations you have at home:

- [ ] Authorised (King James) Version (AV or KJV)
- [ ] Douay Version
- [ ] New International Version (NIV)
- [ ] Revised Standard Version (RSV or New RSV)
- [ ] New American Standard Bible (NASB)
- [ ] Good News for Modern Man (GNB)
- [ ] New King James (Revised AV or NKJV)
- [ ] Jerusalem Bible (JB)
- [ ] The Message
- [ ] The Living Bible (LB)
- [ ] Other versions:

WHICH ONE IS THE ORIGINAL?

If you were to have the original manuscripts of the Bible, you probably couldn't read them anyway. The Old Testament was written mostly in *Hebrew*, with a few passages in *Aramaic*. The New Testament was written in *Greek*. Although none of the original manuscripts survives, there are thousands of early copies. In 1948 a spectacular discovery was made at the Dead Sea; very ancient copies of almost every part of the Old Testament were found. The British Museum and the Chester Beatty Library in Dublin have very ancient copies of the New Testament.

TRANSLATIONS

In order for each people group to read the Word of God for themselves, it had to be *translated* into their own language. At first Latin was the major language, and translations were made into Latin. However, as the centuries moved on and the people spoke other languages, the clergy continued to use only the Latin Bible. It became more and more unfamiliar to ordinary people, until finally whole nations, supposedly Christian, were completely ignorant of its contents. Most people, including the clergy, had a merely formal use of Scripture, and knew little of the transforming power of the Word of God. They were like those religious leaders to whom Jesus said:

You are in error because you do not know the Scriptures or the power of God. (Matthew 22:29)

THE BIBLE IN BRITAIN AND IRELAND

Irish and British Celtic Christians had a particular love for the Bible. They studied and copied the Scriptures in 'Bible Schools' at Glendalough, Iona and Lindisfarne. Some of their work is a highlight of Western Art. See how beautifully they copied the Gospels in the Book of Kells, now at Trinity College Dublin, and in the famous Lindisfarne Gospels at the British Museum. Celtic high crosses are often covered back and front with Bible stories.

Patrick, a Spirit-filled Christian from Britain, was a radical who captured the heart of a whole nation. He loved the scriptures, he knew the power of God, and he preached the new birth to the Irish. *'I will not hesitate to speak of the signs and wonders which God has wrought through me'*, he said. *'Many were born again into God through me in the uttermost part of the world.'* A great company followed in his path: Columba in Scotland, Aidan in England, David in Wales, Columbanus on the Continent. Down the centuries many have given their lives in Britain and Ireland for love of the message you are reading today. When you open your Bible, you are part of a truly great heritage. So, let's help you get to know it better.

WHICH VERSION SHOULD I USE?

English translations may be of several kinds. There is a **word for word** type of translation, which seeks to be as accurate as possible in rendering each Greek or Hebrew word in English. This type is good for study, but can be a bit 'wooden'. A good choice here is the *NASB (New American Standard)*. Most people used to like the *Authorised (King James) Version*, and it has recently been revised as the *'New King James'*. There is also a *New Revised Standard Version*.

Then there is the **paraphrase** which seeks to render the *idea* of a phrase or whole sentence. These are very easy to *read*, but aren't much use for *study*; they just aren't *accurate* enough. They are usually produced by one translator whose own style is very prominent. A really good new paraphrase is *The Message*.

The *New International Version (NIV)* is the most widely used of the modern translations. It gives the equivalent *sense* of the words, while maintaining accuracy and a readable style. This is the version used in these notes. There is an excellent *NIV Study Bible*, also a *Student Bible*.

In your time with the Lord today, read a section from the longest Psalm, 119. It's all about the psalmist's delight in the Word of God. Ask him to nourish the same delight in you for reading, hearing and following God's Word.

week 4
The Word of God

day 3: Reading the Bible for Yourself

Let's look today at *how* to read the Bible. It's not quite like reading any other book, because there isn't any other book whose author lives in you (unless you wrote it yourself)!

It will help you to know how the Bible is *arranged*, so open up the *Contents* page at the very beginning of your Bible.

The first thing you'll see is that the Bible is, in fact, a *collection* of books. There are 66 in all. Your list starts with *Genesis* and ends with *Revelation* (or the *Apocalypse*).

Then you'll notice that there are two major divisions in the Bible. What are they called?

O_____ and N _____

Now, although the list of strange names might seem very complicated, the books are actually arranged in a meaningful order, in several groups. Look at the following 'bookshelf' and you see what the groupings are. Try to learn the major groups in sequence. It will help you find things.

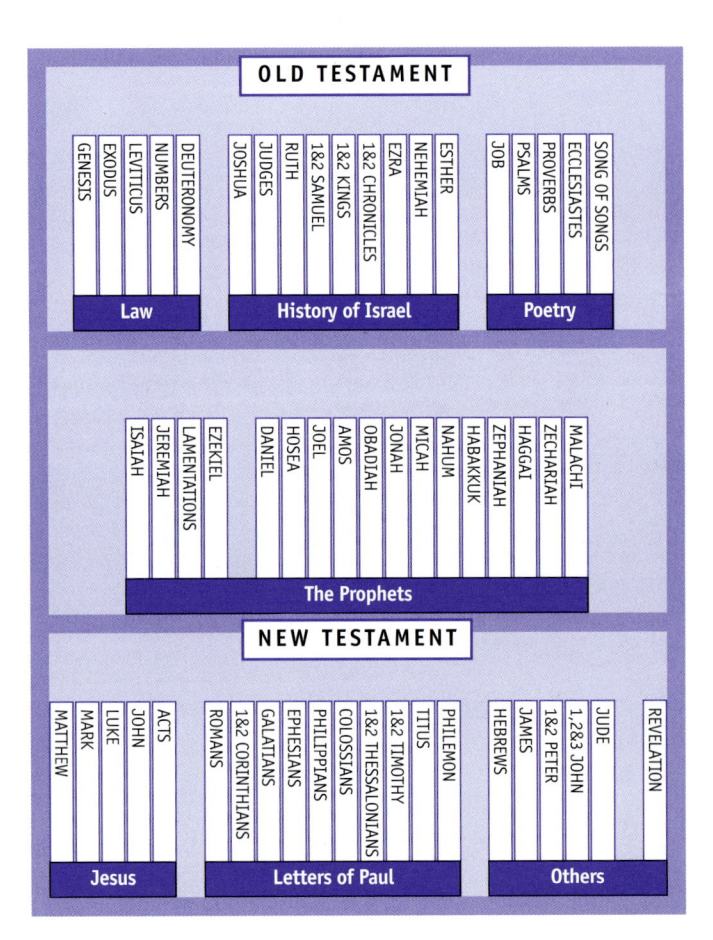

OLD TESTAMENT

Law: GENESIS, EXODUS, LEVITICUS, NUMBERS, DEUTERONOMY

History of Israel: JOSHUA, JUDGES, RUTH, 1&2 SAMUEL, 1&2 KINGS, 1&2 CHRONICLES, EZRA, NEHEMIAH, ESTHER

Poetry: JOB, PSALMS, PROVERBS, ECCLESIASTES, SONG OF SONGS

The Prophets: ISAIAH, JEREMIAH, LAMENTATIONS, EZEKIEL, DANIEL, HOSEA, JOEL, AMOS, OBADIAH, JONAH, MICAH, NAHUM, HABAKKUK, ZEPHANIAH, HAGGAI, ZECHARIAH, MALACHI

NEW TESTAMENT

Jesus: MATTHEW, MARK, LUKE, JOHN

Acts: ACTS

Letters of Paul: ROMANS, 1&2 CORINTHIANS, GALATIANS, EPHESIANS, PHILIPPIANS, COLOSSIANS, 1&2 THESSALONIANS, 1&2 TIMOTHY, TITUS, PHILEMON

Others: HEBREWS, JAMES, 1&2 PETER, 1,2&3 JOHN, JUDE, REVELATION

day 3   Reading the Bible for Yourself

HOW TO STUDY THE BIBLE

You could read the Bible fom the beginning, but it's probably wiser to start with one of the Gospels – let's say *Mark*. You might want to read the whole Gospel first, before studying it *a paragraph at at time*.

Today, however, we want to make it as easy as possible for you to get started. So, as you read a small section, you should ask three questions:

1. **WHAT DOES IT SAY?** Before you ask 'what does this passage mean?' you must observe what it actually says. Who's here? Where is it set? When did this take place? What's happening? Is there a warning, an encouragement, a command? Be a good detective; see what you can find.

2. **WHAT DOES IT MEAN?** To understand what a passage means, we need to know what the words mean. There are some helpful study aids we'll mention in a moment. The meaning may be obvious from the context (the surrounding bits). Words used in the passage are usually mentioned elsewhere in the Bible and explained.

3. **WHAT'S GOD SAYING TO ME NOW?** As you read, ask the Lord what he wants to show you. It may be a word of encouragement, a promise, or something you should do. If it's the latter, follow God's command.

OK, YOUR TURN

So now, take your notebook and make three columns, one for each of our three questions. Choose a paragraph to study. (1 Thessalonians 4:13-18 is one suggestion.) At the end, write here one thing you felt God was saying to you.

STUDY HELPS

There are several basic helps you should purchase when you can afford them. Have a look at someone else's first.
- **English dictionary.** You should have a good one.
- **Dictionary of Bible words.** This explains how words are used in the Bible and is very useful.
- **Concordance.** This is an alphabetical listing of every word in the Bible. It helps you find a particular verse. Some Bibles have a short concordance at the back. If you have a computer, there are free Bible programs that provide a concordance.
- **Bible dictionary or handbook.** This is like a small encyclopaedia of the Bible. *The Illustrated Bible Dictionary* published by IVP is an attractive three-volume set. Also good is the *Lion Handbook of the Bible*.
- **Commentaries** are explanations of the Bible books by modern authors. It would be best not to purchase these just yet.
- **Your fellowship leaders!** Don't forget that God gives teachers to build us up. Take notes, listen to tapes.

week 4
The Word of God

day 4: Spending an Hour in Prayer

Well, how have your times with the Lord been going? Have you spent time with him each day? Do you feel you're growing already? Or has it been a bit of a battle?

If it's been a bit of a struggle to spend time with Jesus, what would you say has been the problem?

- [ ] I don't really know what to do.
- [ ] I'm too busy.
- [ ] I can't really get alone.
- [ ] Something else has become more important.
- [ ] Other:

BACK TO THE QUIET PLACE

Let's have a look again at how we might spend our time with the Lord.

Start with worship. Sing praises to God. Play a praise tape or CD if you like. Worship him until you feel his presence. (By the way, if you have a car, you can worship out loud as you drive along. It's legal.)

Invite the Holy Spirit to come. Thank him that he is your Teacher. Ask him to open your eyes and heart as you read God's Word. Ask him to speak to your heart, and to give you spiritual gifts.

Read your chosen passage for today. If you're reading through a book, such as 1 John, take today's section, and read it through. Remember our three questions?

- _____
- _____
- _____

Write in your spiritual journal whatever the Lord has been saying to you. Set a time when you will follow what God showed you to do.

PRAY

You may not have a long time each day, so you might want to pray for different people each time. Pray blessing into their lives. Pray for them to experience a new level of Kingdom life. Pray for their spiritual protection. Pray for them to be healed, filled with love, joy and peace. Pray for those who don't yet know the Lord Jesus. God loves them and Jesus died to save them. Pray that they would encounter the power of God in their lives.

Write down three people you would like to begin to pray for who don't yet know the Lord. Share this with your helper when you meet this week. Who is he or she praying for?

KEEPING WATCH FOR AN HOUR

When Jesus was praying in the Garden of Gethsemane, overwhelmed to the point of death because of what he was about to face for you and me, *the disciples fell asleep*. Jesus said to Peter:

> *'Simon, are you asleep? Could you not keep watch for one hour?'* (Mark 14:37)

Perhaps once a week on one of the 'free' days, you might consider spending a longer time in prayer. You could start with, say, ten minutes; before long you may find yourself spending a whole hour praying. Here are some additional suggestions:

- Pray for each member of your cell group.
- Pray for the leaders of the fellowship.
- Pray for friends to come and follow Jesus.
- Pray for your area, and for the nation.
- Pray for your family.
- Pray for yourself.

Diary a time now when you'll do this.

Finally, review your memory verse for this week (Hebrews 4:12) and see if you can remember each of the others too. Tomorrow we'll have a look ahead at what's to come.

week 4
The Word of God

day 5: The Way Ahead

CONGRATULATIONS!

Today you end the first stage of your voyage. By completing *Welcome Aboard* you have shown that you are serious about following Jesus. You will be surprised at how much you have already understood and at what has already become part of your spirit.

When you meet with your helper this week make sure he or she signs the completion box on the next page. When your cell group meets next week they'll want to thank the Lord for what's been happening in your life and pray for you.

In this Headway Discipleship Series you are being prepared for the ministry for which Jesus has saved you. So let's have a look at what lies ahead.

MAKING HEADWAY

Now that you have completed Stage 1 of the Headway Discipleship Series, you are ready for the next stage of the journey. As you set sail, your helper will give you a copy of Stage 2 which is entitled *Making Headway*. This book deals with life within the Christian family and the values of God's kingdom. It will guide you through steps to further growth in the things you have already begun to experience, and will introduce you to the development of your spiritual gifts. It is part of your foundational training for your life's ministry. When you have completed *Making Headway,* you will be able to serve as a helper for someone else!

Here's a free look at your *Making Headway* booklet. We hope you'll really enjoy this next part of the journey.

(cover–making headway)

Before you meet your helper this week, have a look back over *Welcome Aboard*. Review your memory verses and anything else you feel you need to clarify.

At this point, a blessing for you is in order, don't you think?

> *May the Lord, who has begun a good work in you, carry it on to completion until the day Jesus returns to present you before God's throne in his eternal Kingdom. Amen! (See Philippians 1:6)*

Note: If you have been completing this booklet on your own and you don't have contact with other local Christians who can help you, you may wish to email any questions or testimonies you might have. Use the various contact details on the first page.